BUFFALO *Country*

America's National Bison Range

Photography by Donald M. Jones

Dedication

To my big brother Greg for taking me to the
National Bison Range for the first time in July, 1972.

Thanks Greg!

Acknowledgments

I would like to thank Pat Jamieson, National Bison Range outdoor recreation planner, for all her support of my photography at the range over the years; it's been invaluable. I would also like to thank National Bison Range project leader Steve Kallin and assistant project leader Bill West for their support in this book project. I hope this book will represent the National Bison Range in the positive and supportive way it well deserves.

Copyright © 2005 by Riverbend Publishing Company

Photographs copyright © 2005 by Donald M. Jones

Published by Riverbend Publishing, Helena, Montana

Printed in the USA.

2 3 4 5 VP 20 19 18 17 16 15

Cover and text design by DD Dowden

ISBN 1-931832-56-0

RIVERBEND PUBLISHING
P.O. Box 5833
Helena, MT 59604
1-866-787-2363
www.riverbendpublishing.com

Contents

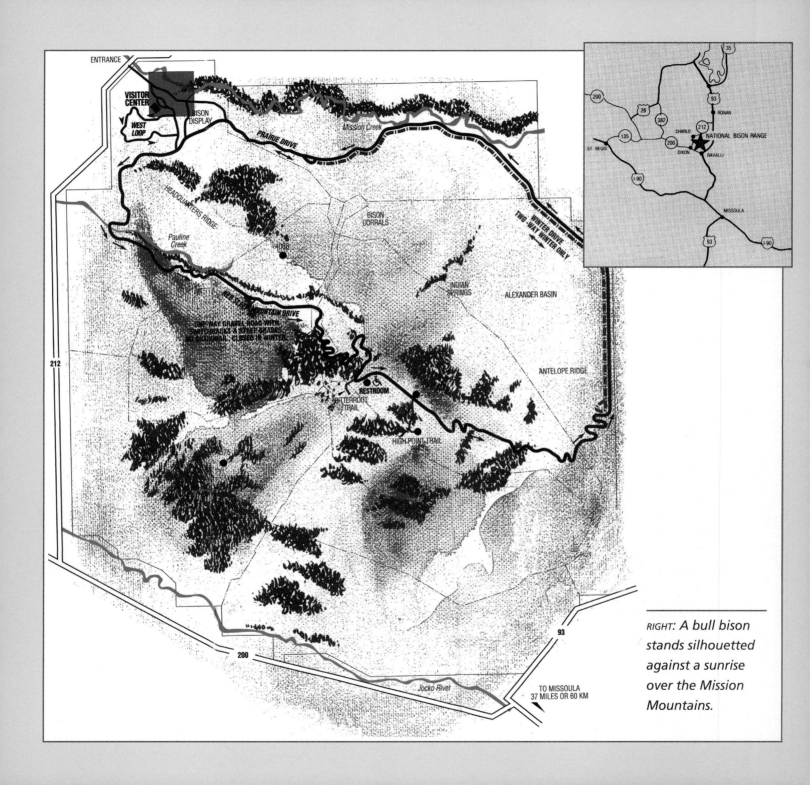

RIGHT: A bull bison stands silhouetted against a sunrise over the Mission Mountains.

Welcome

The National Bison Range protects one of the most important herds of bison in the United States. Located within the beautiful Mission Valley of western Montana, the range supports 300 to 500 bison on nearly 19,000 acres of grasslands, steep hills and waterways. The range also contains elk, two species of deer, pronghorn antelope, bighorn sheep, and hundreds of other animal species. Watching wildlife is the premier activity for visitors.

The highlight of a visit is the 19-mile Red Sleep Mountain self-guided drive. The trip takes about two hours with many opportunities to see wildlife, stop at interpretive displays, and even take short hikes. The impressive 10,000-foot peaks of the Mission Mountains are visible across the Flathead Valley. A shorter tour, the four-mile Buffalo Prairie Drive, is also available.

Both tours begin and end at the visitor center. The center features historical and biological information on bison, ecological displays, and a large, three-dimensional map that shows visitors where to expect to see bison that day. Two nature trails start near the center. Rangers are available to answer questions and help visitors enjoy their stay.

In addition to wildlife viewing, the range offers a day use area with picnic tables and fishing areas. The range is open all year, although portions of the road system are closed in the winter.

The National Bison Range is part of the National Wildlife Refuge System administered by the U.S. Fish and Wildlife Service. It is located within the boundaries of the Flathead Indian Reservation of the Confederated Salish and Kootenai Tribes.

LEFT: In the spring, male blue grouse perform this breeding display to attract females.

FACING PAGE: A large bull elk makes his way down Headquarters Ridge behind the visitor center.

ABOVE: Visitors take time to enjoy the vista and the interpretive displays at the summit of the Red Sleep Mountain Drive.

FACING PAGE: Vehicles on the auto tour make the impressive climb up Elk Lane.

RIGHT: Lazuli buntings can be found throughout the refuge. Pauline Creek is one of the better viewing spots.

FACING PAGE: A mule deer fawn makes its way through a small patch of snowberry.

A cold wind

Prior to the white man's arrival on the North American continent, bison were the most numerous of all grazing animals, numbering between thirty and seventy million animals. Although bison ranged from Oregon to Florida and from Canada to Mexico, the greatest herds were on the plains and prairies between the Rocky Mountains and the Mississippi River.

By 1819 almost all bison east of the Mississippi had been killed. In the 1830s fur companies began to purchase bison skins to supplement the dwindling supply of beaver pelts. More and more bison were killed so their skins could be traded for firearms, gunpowder, textiles, and other goods.

The wholesale slaughter of bison on the Great Plains peaked in the years following the Civil War. During this time the ecology of the American West was radically changed by a large influx of white settlers. New railroad lines carried large numbers of people to the plains in search of inexpensive land, gold, and new opportunities. In turn, the railroads carried tons of bison hides back east. Bison hunters, such as William "Buffalo Bill" Cody,

RIGHT: *Yellow-headed blackbirds are commonly seen along the nature trail during the spring and summer.*

FACING PAGE: *Buffalo slaughter by hide hunters on the Montana plains, 1880.*

earned their living by killing bison for their hides or to feed railroad workers. Many bison were killed for their tongues alone, which were considered a delicacy. Some government officials also justified bison hunting as a way to subdue the Plains Indians by destroying their primary source of food, clothing, and shelter.

In the early 1870s a new hide tanning process was developed, and hunting bison solely for their hides became very profitable. In 1872, two million bison were killed for their hides, which sold for about $3.50 each. As many as 250 bison could be shot in one day by one hunter, and a good skinner could remove a hide in five minutes. Between 1868 and 1881 an estimated thirty-one million bison were killed.

Previously protected by its remote location, the huge northern herd in central Montana was the last of the great herds to fall. Hide shipments down the Missouri River from Fort Benton peaked at 80,000 hides in 1876, the same year Custer was defeated at the Battle of the Little Bighorn in southeastern Montana. By 1884 there were no more hides to ship. Sitting Bull, the Sioux chief who defeated Custer, said, "A cold wind blew across the prairie when the last buffalo fell … a death-wind for my people."

The bison were nearly exterminated. The grunts and roars of the bison that played across the Great Plains for 15,000 years were gone. By 1889 there were less than 1,000 bison in the United States. In 1902 only one wild herd remained in the entire country, a group of twenty-three animals in the remote backcountry of Yellowstone National Park.

Even as bison were being killed, some Americans were calling for their preservation. Concerned citizens lobbied for game laws and wildlife refuges. Perhaps most importantly, Theodore Roosevelt became president in 1901.

Roosevelt's passion for wildlife and wild lands led to the creation of the national forests and national wildlife refuges, and additional national parks. Roosevelt signed the bill that created the National Bison Range in 1908. As described in the next chapter, this action was one of the most important steps in saving North American bison.

A pronghorn antelope stands alert at sunrise.

LEFT: Though mule deer may be found throughout the refuge, most visitors see them at the higher elevations of the tour route.

BELOW: Alert, reclusive, and often hidden by tall grass, badgers are rarely seen.

Bison Hunting by Native Americans

Native Americans hunted bison during all seasons. As bison moved onto the open plains during the warmer months and then back to sheltered valleys and wooded areas during winter, the Indians followed them, changing their hunting methods to match the terrain.

Though killing such large, fast animals was a formidable task, ancient tribes soon perfected several effective techniques. Before the arrival of horses, Indians hunted bison on foot, disguising themselves under the pelts of wolves and other animals the bison did not fear. They also used a technique called the "surround" where they surrounded a herd until they got close enough to shoot arrows and throw spears. In wooded areas, Indians used a technique called the "impound" where they would drive bison into hidden corrals and kill them at close distances. The most famous method was the "buffalo jump" or "pishkun." Hunters would stampede an entire herd over cliffs or bluffs up to 250 feet high. The animals would fall into a corral where those that had not been killed by the fall would be killed with clubs, spears, knives, and arrows. There are several pishkun sites in Montana.

Hunting was a man's responsibility. The task of butchering fell either to men or women, depending upon the tribe. The meat was usually distributed according to tribal customs. As a result, no one went hungry. The women and young girls tanned the hides and prepared the meat. Most of the meat was preserved for the future, dried as jerky or made into pemmican. Some of the meat, once dried, was stored in caches to be retrieved at a later time. The two biggest influences on bison hunting were the introduction of the horse in the 1600s and the repeating rifle in the 1870s. Hunting on horseback was so effective that some other techniques, such as the impound, were abandoned.

Regardless of the changes in hunting methods, Indians never threatened the great herds with extinction. Although at times Indians may have killed large numbers of animals, nothing affected the enormous free-ranging bison herds more than the settlement of the West by the white man.

Bison graze on a hillside while the Mission Mountains loom in the background.

Going to buffalo

Bison hunting was a way of life for Native Americans on both sides of the Rocky Mountains. Of course, many tribes lived with the bison on the Great Plains, but tribes living in the forests west of the mountains also hunted bison. These tribes made two or three trips to the plains each year and each trip took many months. Sometimes a tribe stayed on the plains for a year, making meat and taking robes, before returning home. These grand pilgrimages were called "going to buffalo."

Men, women, and children, along with countless dogs and thousands of horses, trekked up rivers that flowed from the Rockies. They gathered in the Bitterroot and Clark Fork valleys in western Montana to prepare for crossing the mountains and to make strategic alliances with other tribes. The alliances were necessary to defend themselves from the Blackfeet and other plains tribes.

Several routes led across the mountains. Many routes were so wide and well worn that early fur traders described them as roads. The Blackfoot River southeast of the National Bison Range was called "the river of the road to the buffalo."

These trips were long, arduous, and dangerous, but the benefits of "going to buffalo" outweighed all risks. A successful hunt meant enough meat to sustain a tribe for months. It meant hides for a hundred uses, including trade. It meant excitement and adventure. For these reasons, "going to buffalo" remained an important tradition until the bison herds were gone.

An adult bull bison and a yearling walk the prairie as a summer storm approaches.

How the parts of a buffalo were used by Native Americans

The bison was the Native Americans' all-purpose supply store. Here are just some of the uses of bison.

Food

Fresh and dried meat from the muscles

Fresh meat from the tongue, brains, heart, liver, intestines

Fat and bone marrow

Hides

Clothing, including robes, shirts, leggings, dresses, belts, mittens, hats, moccasins.

Teepees

Blankets

Rugs

Shields

Bags, pouches, and buckets

Pack gear for horses and dogs

Boats

Game items, such as covers for balls

Hooves

Glue

Ceremonial rattles, masks

Dung

Fuel

Signs, markers

Bones

Tools such as knives, scrapers, hoes, sewing awls

Arrowheads, lance points

Sled runners (from ribs)

Clothing ornaments

Counters in gambling games

Horns

Eating utensils such as spoons and cups

Containers for gunpowder

Ceremonial headdresses, masks

Hair

Rope

Brushes

Ornaments for clothing, tepees, weapons

Stuffing for balls used in games

Fly whisks (from the tails)

Sinew

Twine and thread

Bowstrings

Arrowhead wrappings

Organs

Brains and liver for tanning hides

Rough side of tongues for hairbrushes

Pouches and bags from bladders, intestines, stomachs

A bull bison has shed nearly its entire winter coat.

BELOW: Many visitors love to have their picture taken in front of this massive pile of elk antlers next to the visitor center. The shed antlers have been collected on the range over many years.

FACING PAGE: Elk feed lazily on an open hillside on a September morning.

Creating the National Bison Range

As one story goes, in 1873 or 1874 Samuel Walking Coyote, a Pend d'Oreille, returned to the Flathead Indian Reservation in Montana with four orphaned bison calves, two bulls and two cows, after spending the winter with the Blackfeet tribe east of the Continental Divide. Ironically, Walking Coyote returned along the "going to buffalo" route that Salish-speaking peoples had used for hundreds of years to reach the bison hunting grounds of the plains. Walking Coyote raised the bison at his place on the Flathead River near Dixon, and the herd slowly increased.

In 1884 Walking Coyote sold his herd, numbering twelve or thirteen animals, to Charles Allard, Sr., and Michel Pablo, cattle ranchers on the reservation who were married to tribal members. In 1893 they bought twenty-six bison from Charles "Buffalo" Jones, a former buffalo hunter and bison rancher from Kansas. Jones later became the game warden responsible for protecting the bison herd at Yellowstone National Park.

In 1896 Allard died and the herd was divided equally among family members. At that time fewer than 1,000 bison remained anywhere, and the Pablo/Allard herd was the largest herd in existence. In 1899 Allard's wife sold some animals to Charles Conrad, a rancher and businessman of nearby Kalispell, Montana. Pablo retained his herd but faced increasing difficulties. Reservation lands were being sold to white settlers, and the settlers erected fences, restricting the herd's mobility. Poaching increased. Seeing the inevitable loss of his bison, Pablo tried to sell his herd to the federal government.

Bison have average vision, good hearing, and an excellent sense of smell.

President Theodore Roosevelt lobbied Congress for funds for a bison refuge but was rebuffed. Instead, the Canadian government purchased Pablo's two hundred head in 1907 to reintroduce bison into its vast prairies.

The sale of this last, large herd out of the country produced a huge public outcry. William Hornaday, head of the New York Zoological Society and author of a popular book on the bison's extermination, helped found the American Bison Society. The society rallied public support for a bison refuge where bison could reproduce under natural conditions, protected from hunters.

Having collected bison specimens in Montana for the Smithsonian Institution, Hornaday believed Montana was an ideal site for a bison refuge. With support of the society, Montana Senator Joseph M. Dixon, who had been instrumental in opening up the Flathead Reservation to white settlers, introduced a bill to the 1908 Congress to establish a bison range in his home state.

Perhaps embarrassed by Canada's willingness to buy American bison and certainly pressured by the public, Congress passed the bill, and

Both male and female pronghorn antelope have horns, but the male's horns, as shown here, are much larger.

Roosevelt immediately signed it on May 23, 1908. On June 15, 1909, 18,521 acres on the Flathead Reservation were purchased from the Salish, Kootenai and Pend d'Oreille tribes for about $29,000. This purchase created the range under the management of the Bureau of Biological Survey, which later became the U.S. Fish and Wildlife Service. It was the first time the federal government had purchased land for no other reason than to protect wildlife.

The American Bison Society raised $10,056 through public donations throughout the nation to purchase thirty-four bison from the Conrad herd. These animals and an animal donated by famous rancher Charles Goodnight of Texas formed the original herd for the range.

The first bison were released into the range on October 17, 1909. "As the crates were opened," Hornaday wrote, "the animals backed out of them, looked about for a moment, saw their Paradise Regained looming up on the farther side of the Jocko River, splashed across the stream, and climbed into their new home." Appropriately, most of these bison were descendents of the four bison calves that Walking Coyote had brought from the plains.

A short-eared owl tries a different way of looking at things. Five species of owls can be found year-round on the range.

More animals for the range

Only a year after the first bison were released into the range, pronghorn antelope and white-tailed deer were added. Elk were released in 1911, mule deer in 1918, and bighorn sheep in 1922. These animals came from various sources, including the Boone and Crockett Club of New York, Yellowstone National Park, the city of Missoula, Montana, and the Canadian National Parks Service.

ABOVE: White-tailed deer are common along the nature trail.
PHOTO BY LUKE A. JONES

LEFT: Bighorn sheep are most often found while traveling down the tour route from the high point.

Bison country today

Establishing the National Bison Range was one of this country's most important steps in saving bison and helping the species recover. As the range herd increased, surplus animals from the range were used to start herds in other places.

Today there are 20,000 to 25,000 bison in public herds. The largest herd, numbering several thousand animals, is in Yellowstone National Park.

Other large public herds are found at Badlands and Wind Cave national parks and Custer State Park in South Dakota; at Theodore Roosevelt National Park in North Dakota; at Witchita Mountains Wildlife Refuge in Oklahoma; at Fort Niobrara National Wildlife Refuge and Fort Robinson State Park in Nebraska; at Antelope Island and the Henry Mountains in Utah; at Delta Junction in Alaska, and at the National Elk Refuge/Grand Teton National Park in Wyoming.

There are also more than 300,000 bison on private ranches today.

LEFT: Bison calves are born from mid-April to mid-May. Born light chocolate in color, they will grow the dark coat of an adult by their first autumn.

FACING PAGE: Here is an early summer view of Elk Creek from just before the high point of the tour route.

The roundup

Every fall the National Bison Range conducts a bison roundup. The range can support about 380 bison over the winter. Since nearly ninety percent of mature bison cows have calves every spring, the roundup is used to keep the bison population in balance with the habitat. The roundup also allows range managers to monitor the herd's health.

The roundup is an exciting event, and it is open to the public. Cowboys on horseback round up the bison and herd them towards a network of strong corrals and holding pens, where the animals are sorted, weighed, and tested for health.

Surplus animals have provided breeding stock for many bison herds across the country. Bison are transferred to other parks or used in research programs. Bison are also provided to Native American

tribes to establish herds on tribal lands. All bison not used for other government herds, research, or tribes are sold to the public through sealed bids. A mix of bulls and cows are sold. In deciding which animals to sell, the primary consideration is to maintain the proper composition of ages and sexes in the range herd. Usually about 60 to 80 animals are sold or donated each year.

The roundup takes a lot of preparation but only lasts two days. Animals that are sold may be kept in holding pens for a few days for health tests, but the herd animals are released back onto the range.

LEFT: During the annual bison roundup, visitors enjoy close-up views of bison and bison management.

RIGHT: To sort, weigh, and examine animals during the roundup, bison are moved through a series of reinforced chutes and corrals.

Big Medicine 1933-1959

White bison are extremely rare, historically appearing only once in every five million births. To many Indian peoples such animals are sacred and represent great spiritual power. Consequently, the May 3, 1933, birth of a white buffalo calf on the National Bison Range was greeted with celebration and wonder. People began referring to the calf as Big Medicine in recognition of the sacred power attributed to white bison by Native American people.

Because he had some pigmentation—blue eyes, tan hooves, and a brown topknot—Big Medicine was a white buffalo rather than a pure albino. He was born of a cow and bull of normal color. He sired one albino calf that was sent to the National Zoological Gardens in Washington, D.C.

At his prime, Big Medicine weighed 1,900 pounds, stood six feet high at the hump, and measured twelve feet from the tip of his nose to the end of his tail. Although his fame spread worldwide, Big Medicine spent his entire life on the National Bison Range where he received special care that enabled him to live much longer than bison normally do.

Because Big Medicine held great significance for the people of Montana, both Native American and non-Indian, the Montana Historical Society made a life-sized mount from the hide when he died of old age in 1959. The mount of Big Medicine is now on permanent display at the society's museum in Helena.

---

*FACING PAGE: **Big Medicine on the National Bison Range.***

The bison's life

Bison are strong, hardy, nomadic grazers, built to thrive on vast grasslands swept by strong winds, searing heat, and deep snows.

Despite their slow walking gait, bison are surprisingly fast and agile for animals that weigh more than half a ton. They can run as fast as a horse, jump as high as a deer, and swim as well as a dog. They are strong enough to break through fences and nimble enough to scale steep slopes. They have great endurance and can travel dozens of miles without stopping. They can maintain a gallop for longer distances than a horse.

Bison are herd animals, with cows, young animals, and some bulls forming large groups throughout the year. In historic times, herds could number hundreds of thousands of animals. Large, older bulls often live much of the year in smaller bachelor herds. They join the cows during the breeding season, or rut, which takes place in July and August.

The largest bulls may weigh 2,000 pounds or more. The average weight is about 1,600 pounds. They can be six feet tall at the shoulder and measure 12 feet from the tip of their noses to the end of their tails. Bulls have heavy horns and a large shoulder hump of muscle that supports their enormous head and thick skull. They have a thick mass of fur on their heads and a heavily furred front cape, even during the summer. This enhances their size and protects them when fighting other bulls during the breeding season. Bulls are notoriously agitated and ill tempered during the rut, and while the fighting can be fierce, deaths are rare. Bulls challenge each other with loud roars that echo across the grasslands.

Cows weigh about half as much as bulls. They have smaller humps and a smoother summer coat. Their horns are narrower. Horns on older females almost meet above their heads.

Calves are born from mid-April through May and weigh from 25 to 40 pounds. They are able to travel with their mothers within three hours of birth. Calves are reddish in color until about three months of age, when

Bison like to rub against trees, boulders—and road signs.

they grow the dark brown coat of an adult. Cows usually have a single calf. They are very protective of their young and can be more dangerous than a bull when they have a calf at their side. Calves grow rapidly and within one year may weigh from 400 to 600 pounds.

Buffalo horns are not shed annually like antlers but grow larger each year. Horns can be lethal weapons against predators, and bulls may show scars from horns after fights with other bulls. Bison have been known to use their horns to toss elk and even other buffalo several feet in the air.

A bison's heavy coat protects it from both summer sun and winter winds. The thick winter coat is such good insulation that snow lies on their backs and heads without melting. In winter, bison use their large heads like brooms to push aside snow and expose grass to eat.

Bison shed their winter fur in the spring, often accelerating the itchy process by wallowing or rubbing vigorously against large

RIGHT: *A mature bison may stand six feet tall at its shoulder.*

FACING PAGE: *Bison calves practice head butting, a serious activity for mature bulls during the breeding season.*

boulders and trees. When telegraph poles were erected across the frontier West, bison would rub against the poles and knock them over. Sharp spikes were added to discourage rubbing, but the spikes only made the poles more useful to the bison.

Bison feed on grass by tearing it rather than biting it off. Like domestic cattle, bison are ruminants, meaning they regurgitate their food and chew it a second time. This process efficiently utilizes nutrition from grasses and other high fiber foods. Bison may live up to 30 years, but the average life span is 15 to 20 years.

In the summer, bison paw certain areas to create large depressions of bare dirt. Bison lie down and roll in these areas, called wallows, to coat their bodies with dust, which helps alleviate the irritations of biting insects.

Bison have average eyesight, good hearing, and a great sense of smell. Early explorers said bison could smell water from miles away and locate thick grass buried beneath a foot of snow.

Bison suffer few diseases in the wild. The brucellosis attributed to bison herds today, especially in Yellowstone National Park, is really a cattle disease that was transmitted to bison. After a series of testing and management actions in the 1940s and 1950s, the Bison Range herd has been certified brucellosis-free.

A healthy mature bison has little to fear. In wild environments, wolves and grizzly bears sometimes prey on the old, young, injured, and sick, and newborn calves can also be vulnerable to coyotes and mountain lions.

Be careful!

Bison are strong and unpredictable, and they can be dangerous. Give them plenty of room and do not approach them. A bison's tail is often a handy warning flag. When it hangs down and is switching naturally, the animal usually is unperturbed. If it extends out straight and droops at the end, the animal is becoming mildly agitated. If the tail is sticking straight up, they are ready to charge and you should be somewhere else...but do not run or they might chase you!

LEFT: All bison, even a younger one like this one, should be watched from the safety of a car.

FACING PAGE: Usually found along streams, white-tailed deer sometimes use the range's higher, open habitat.

LEFT: The smallest owl on the range, the pygmy owl measures a mere six inches in length.

FACING PAGE: A whitetail buck stands at attention in a tall stand of teasel.

LEFT: Canada geese rest on the pond along the nature trail.

BELOW: Pronghorn antelope can run faster than sixty miles an hour.

FACING PAGE: Great horned owls nest in cottonwood trees along Mission Creek and can often be seen from the nature trail.

The homes on the range

A̲ll species of animals and plants need certain combinations of food, water, cover, and space in order to live and reproduce. Together these elements make up their habitat. The rich diversity of wildlife on the National Bison Range is evidence of its rich diversity of habitats. The range supports four major habitat types: grasslands, mountain forests, riparian zones, and wetlands. Some animals depend on one specific habitat but most animals utilize more than one type of habitat for different daily needs or during different seasons.

GRASSLANDS

Though grasslands may appear monotonous, they form a vibrant ecosystem. The range grasslands are classified as Palouse prairie, and the primary grasses are Idaho fescue, rough fescue, and bluebunch wheatgrass. These native grasses are called bunch grasses because they grow in clumps, with the dense crown of grass providing shelter and protection for the roots underneath. While most plants grow from the tips of their branches or stems, these grasses grow at the base of their stems. This adaptation allows them to continue to grow even after their tops have been grazed off. Grasslands also contain broad-leaved plants called forbs. Many forbs are wildflowers.

Grasslands support grazing animals such as bison and pronghorn antelope, and a variety of birds, rodents, and predators such as the coyote and badger.

FACING PAGE: A magnificent bull bison in his prime.

RIGHT: Hungarian partridge may be encountered all along the tour route but rarely do they pose like this family.

Mountain forests

Douglas firs and ponderosa pines cover the tops of the hills of the Bison Range. With dry conditions (only 13 inches of precipitation each year), this area is on the edge of forest survival, and tree growth is largely regulated by moisture. Trees grow at higher elevations where it is cooler and moister, on cooler north slopes, and where depressions hold moisture.

Western tanagers are one of many species of neo-tropic songbirds that migrate to the range each spring.

Birds of the mountain forest eat pine nuts, new buds, seeds, and berries plus insects that live in the bark and wood. Since most of these things are available all year, many forest birds such as chickadees, jays, and woodpeckers do not migrate. Other animals use the forest for shade in the summer and protection from the cold in the winter. Deer and elk browse on woodland plants.

More often heard than seen, marsh wrens call from cattails along Mission Creek and adjacent ponds.

Life is most abundant along the range's riparian areas where white-tailed deer, elk, mink, and turtles can be regularly seen.

RIPARIAN ZONES

The lush growth of vegetation along a stream is caused by moisture from the stream seeping into the ground around it. These streamside thickets, called riparian zones, have an appearance and a microclimate very different from the surrounding grasslands. They have thicker vegetation, more shade, higher humidity, and increased air movement. There are several streams on the Bison Range that support riparian zones, especially Mission Creek along the north side and Jocko River along the south side.

Riparian zones provide very good wildlife habitat. Fish, insects and other creatures live in the flowing water. Birds find abundant food and protective shelter for nesting. Deer, elk and bison drink the water and forage on the lush plant growth. Mink, otters, and raccoons prefer the waterways for hunting and foraging. Even black bears like to feed on berries that grow in these areas.

WETLANDS

Wetlands form in any depression where water collects. They may be marshes, bogs, swamps, ponds, potholes, or old river bends separated from the main channel. Wetlands are very important. They hold water so it can seep down and recharge the aquifer. They filter pollutants and sediments from the water and help control floods and erosion. Wetlands produce the greatest food volume of any environment and provide habitat for waterfowl and many other kinds of wildlife. Numerous species of birds nest near wetlands because of the abundant supply of insects.

FACING PAGE: *Otters never seem to stay in one place very long. They move up and down Mission Creek in search of a good fish dinner.*

RIGHT: *During late summer and early fall, black bears like to feed on hawthorn berries along Pauline Creek.*

Winter on the range

Winter puts a whole new edge on animal survival. Many food sources dry up; others are buried under deep snow. Temperatures are bitterly cold. Animals of the Bison Range handle winter in a variety of ways: they migrate, hibernate, adapt, or endure.

Animals prepare for winter by growing heavier fur. Some animals such as jackrabbits and weasels grow white fur to hide better in the snow.

Some animals continue to find their usual foods such as seeds or browse. Meadow voles make tunnels under the snow and forage along the ground as always. Deer eat twigs that are higher than the snow level. Birds eat berries and seeds they can find above the snow. Small animals such as rabbits reach higher bushes as the snow depth increases. Elk and bison find exposed grass on wind-swept ridges or paw through snow for grasses and forbs.

Creatures that cannot find winter foods must migrate or hibernate. Ground squirrels hibernate. This requires locating or digging an underground den and growing a layer of fat to sustain them through the winter. Many birds migrate, and they must grow fat reserves for their long trips to wintering grounds.

Cold temperatures require a sizeable supply of heat-producing foods just to keep warm, and deep snow increases the amount of energy required to move from place to place. Therefore any disturbance causing an animal to flee, or even to remain alert because of an intrusion, can use up more energy and threaten its survival.

The longer and colder the winter, the more difficult it is to survive. Animals may use up their layers of fat. Snow may become too deep to paw through or move through to find food. All animals become weaker, providing food for the predators that feed on the weak. Some animals die. But winter always ends, and spring brings food and warmth.

Spring arrives at the range with the birth of bison calves, even if the Mission Mountains remain gripped by winter.

ABOVE: *A bald eagle soars along Mission Creek. Both bald and golden eagles can be found year-round on the range.*

RIGHT: *Though very rarely seen, mountain lions are residents of the range and play a key role in the balance between predator and prey.* PHOTO BY JIM HUESTES

*Well insulated by heavy
fur, bison seem unfazed by
winter's cold and snow.*

LEFT: A large mule deer buck with antlers freshly out of velvet stands in a morning sunbeam.

FACING PAGE: The 19,000-acre range features a variety of habitats from streams to grass prairies to timbered hills.

RIGHT: Mountain bluebirds can be spotted all along the tour route in the spring and summer.

BELOW: Mule deer alert and watching.

FACING PAGE: The bitterroot, Montana's state flower, is found fairly easily along the Bitterroot Trail in June.

LEFT: A red-tailed hawk screams as if to warn all intruders to stay away.

BELOW: A cow elk feeds in thick vegetation along Mission Creek.

FACING PAGE: A whitetail fawn emerges from the undergrowth along Mission Creek.

RIGHT: *Montana's state bird, the western meadowlark is common throughout the range.*

FACING PAGE: *In the spring, the range may look like it is painted yellow because of the thousands upon thousands of arrow-leaf balsamroot flowers.*

Wildlife refuges administered by the National Bison Range

The National Bison Range staff administers nearby Ninepipe and Pablo national wildlife refuges as well as two other refuges and several waterfowl production areas. Each of these areas provides excellent wildlife viewing and photo opportunities for waterfowl and other water birds. For more information on these areas, contact the National Bison Range.

Ninepipe National Wildlife Refuge, 2,062 acres

Location: Within the boundaries of the Flathead Indian Reservation about five miles south of Ronan, Montana.
Description: Primarily a refuge and breeding ground for birds, especially waterfowl. Consists of a 1,672-acre reservoir, numerous smaller ponds and pothole wetlands, and some grassland. Surrounded by state and tribal grasslands.
Recreation: Fishing (largemouth bass), photography, wildlife watching, particularly birds. There is a wildlife viewing area off Highway 93 with an accessible trail, interpretive panels, and pit toilets. The viewing area is jointly managed by the U.S. Fish and Wildlife Service, the Montana Department of Fish, Wildlife and Parks, and the Confederated Salish and Kootenai Tribes.

Pablo National Wildlife Refuge, 2,542 acres

Location: Within the boundaries of the Flathead Indian Reservation about two miles south of Polson, Montana.
Description: Primarily a refuge and breeding ground for birds, especially waterfowl. Consists of a 1,850-acre reservoir, pothole wetlands, and 692 acres of grasslands.
Recreation: Fishing (largemouth bass), photography, wildlife watching, particularly birds. No visitor facilities.

Swan River National Wildlife Refuge, 1,568 acres

Location: In the Swan Valley about 38 miles southeast of Creston, Montana.
Description: Primarily a sanctuary for migratory birds. Consists mainly of sloughs and grass wetlands in the floodplain of the Swan River, plus riparian forests.
Recreation: Fishing on Swan River, photography, wildlife watching, particularly birds, and waterfowl hunting. Wildlife viewing platform with interpretive panels at a parking area.

Lost Trail National Wildlife Refuge, 7,885 acres

Location: In Pleasant Valley about 40 miles west of Kalispell, Montana.

Description: Primarily a sanctuary for migratory birds. Consists mainly of a small lake, wet meadows, prairie grasslands, and wooded slopes.
Recreation: Wildlife watching, photography, hunting for deer, elk, turkey, and forest grouse. Has a headquarters/contact station with restroom facilities open part of the week.

Northwest Montana Wetland Management District, 14,757 total acres in 14 waterfowl production areas and one conservation easement program

Location: Lake and Flathead counties, Montana.
Description: Primarily for migratory birds. Wetlands and grasslands.
Recreation: Wildlife watching, photography, waterfowl and upland bird hunting.

Educational opportunities at the range

The National Bison Range is an excellent area for outdoor education for students and teachers of all grades and expertise. During the school year, teachers visiting the range may request an orientation program for their students. This can consist of a 14-minute general video, other videos about natural history and geology, demonstrations using the skull and skin collection, and activities relating to classroom lesson plans. The accessible nature trail near Mission Creek is superb for riparian and wetland studies. There is also an accessible trail through the grassland near the visitor center. Equipment, activity packets, and field guides are available for use by teachers at these areas.

The Bison Range houses an extensive Environmental Education Library and materials are available to educators for two-week loan period. The library contains substantial reference materials, student activity lesson plans, videos, and field kits which approach environmental education from a variety of subject areas. These items are tailored to subject and grade levels.

The Bison Range hosts one to two teacher workshops per year. Participants can receive Montana Office of Public Instruction credits for all workshops. The workshops emphasize hands-on activities for students in grades K-12.

Contact information

National Bison Range
Refuge Manager
132 Bison Range Road
Moiese, MT 59824
Phone 406-644-2211
Internet: http://bisonrange.fws.gov/nbr/
Email: bisonrange@fws.gov

RIGHT: *The western kingbird perches on fence lines and tree branches, where it watches for insects to fly after and grab out of the air.*

FACING PAGE: *Two mule deer bucks sport new and growing antlers in early summer.*

About the photographer

Don Jones resides in the small northwestern Montana town of Troy with his wife Tess and their two sons, Jake and Luke. Don has been a full-time wildlife photographer for more than a decade with credits including *Field & Stream, Ranger Rick, Sierra, Audubon,* and *Montana Magazine,* to name just a few. He is the photographer of the books *Montana Wildlife Portfolio* and *Rocky Mountain Elk Portfolio. Buffalo Country* is Don's first book with Riverbend Publishing. To learn more about Don and his work, please log on to his web site www.donaldmjones.com.

Photographer Don Jones "editing" his work in the field.